LOGOGRAPHY

A POETRY OMNIBUS

CONFESSIONS II, LYRIC/RESISTANCE, & THE ART OF LOVE

ANIS SHIVANI

Sagging Meniscus

Set in Fournier with LaTeX.

ISBN: 978-1-944697-73-0 (paperback)
Library of Congress Control Number: 2018967214

Sagging Meniscus Press
saggingmeniscus.com

For Mehnaaz

CONTENTS

Acknowledgments *vii*

Confessions II *1*

Lyric/Resistance *103*

The Art of Love *207*

About the Author *295*

Acknowledgments

Many thanks to the editors of *West Branch*, *Seattle Review*, *Asian American Literary Review*, *Tenderloin*, *The Ilanot Review*, and *Mudlark* for publishing individual poems in this collection. My gratitude above all to Jacob Smullyan, publisher of Sagging Meniscus Press, for taking a chance on this challenging volume and bringing it to fruition with his patient shepherding and brilliant insights. My thanks also to Royce M. Becker for designing the book; I have long been a fan of hers, and never imagined that our paths would cross in this felicitous manner and that I would end up with this striking cover. Thanks to Fu and after him Foolittle for being my poetic inspirations, and to my mother who—unbeknownst to me when I was writing *Lyric/Resistance*—was really the inspiration behind the book, and who died shortly after its completion. Some of the material in this book, particularly the middle section of *The Art of Love*, is what is conventionally called "found poetry," but I have come to believe, as a matter of aesthetic principle, that it is neither necessary nor useful to acknowledge such sources of "appropriation." If I were to start doing that, perhaps every line of "poetry" I write might have to be accompanied with footnotes. And who wants to read footnotes, when one can enjoy poetry? I also want to offer deep gratitude to my friends Richard Burgin, Muneeza Shamsie, Harvey L. Hix, Dave Brinks, David Leavitt, Clayton Eshleman, Joe Philips, Susan Wood, Geoffrey Gatza, Gloria Mindock, Jim Magnuson, Kim Davis, Mohsin Hamid, Orhan Pamuk, and the late Franz Wright and his wife Elizabeth Oehlkers Wright, for their years of support and encouragement. Thanks also to Wendy Chin-Tanner, Ali Eteraz, Claudia Keelan, Marilyn Hacker, Campbell McGrath, Fady Joudah, Kevin Prufer, Jay Parini, Rebecca Seiferle, Nick Twemlow, Ifeanyi Menkiti, Kwame Dawes, Ashley Strosnider, Ravi Shankar, Pierre Joris, G. C. Waldrep, Archana Vemulapalli, Usha Akella, Susan Lewis, Cindy Huyser, Manasi Subramaniam, George Witte, Chaitali Sen, and many other friends around the country who have shared thoughts and ideas about poetry over the years. And to my literary friends in Houston, particularly Michael Woodson, Dustin Pickering, Ben Rybeck, Nancy Wozny, Robert Clark, Matt Riley, Dave Cowen, Gary Rosin, Laura Pena, Daniel Carrington, Chris Wise, Fran Sanders, Stephen Gros, Winston Derden, Bucky Rea, Mike McGuire, Shannon McKirchey, Carrie Kornacki, Saba Hussain, Gabrielle Langley, Dean Liscum, Gemini Wahhaj, Elora Shehabuddin, Siddiqur Rahman, Maha Rahman, Dom Zuccone, Mike Alexander, James Adams, Gerald Cedillo, Glenn Burns, Varsha Saraiya-Shah, Stalina Villareal, and Doni Wilson, thanks for the camaraderie. And finally, to the one who revived my interest in poetry more than fifteen years ago, reciting in our very first conversation the poem "Suranjana" by Jibananda Das, including these lines, which I repeat to her: "You are the same magnificent night of sea wailing for the dead / You loved with your entire body yet you love the dawn's delight."

Confessions II

I

Diet of which flathead, edible, leak-
proof pietàs are evidence: in the piece
where I recapture the stress of vending
and walking at the same time (in the booth
where we take hickory-shaded pictures),
you have the tone of the manual to Par-
nassus. Grampus, sit in my lap: near gales,
sounding like skank, are all the more uncon-
vincing because of the silence of cou-
lisses we used to bait in the early days.

2

The bullmastiff came to me and sniffed at
my leveling rods, legs made of nullifid-
ian credit, overwhelmed by the consis-
tency of realists: everywhere I look there
are bottle trees foregoing the greenery
of Mayakovsky. I went after the demons
with their predilection for chastity:
have a seat in this banana republic
you have created from anecdotage and
Moabite pamphlets and renunciation.

3

We are true believers in sectionalism.
The secrets of dentelles, clutch appear-
ances of coastlines in the dreamy lucent
low German you speak in ripcords: do you
fragment into pieces of dehiscence
when I'm not looking? Our favorite commu-
nity college has a circumference of
lamplight restrooms. I like to hide in spheres
of third eyelids, do things with goombays, dance
at the docks with my covenant of nouns.

4

What is privilege? What is the nuisance of
private parts, razorfish, rough timber, snow
plows, homographs, higher criticism?
I was around in the days of leveraged
buyouts, I knew levies on oversleep,
I fed my Siamese cat continental drift.
We will meet next month in carmine birthmarks,
we will excavate our left brains of mimes
left scattered by sex symbols and northern
blots. Speak to me in Ibero-Romance!

5

When we drown we do so in side issues,
year after year the stationary engine
starved of the air fed by the truce that never
comes. War baby, who are the wolves you know
best? I put on my homburg, walk down the
street with my dumb cane, feeling congested
with cloth. At the cantina my past in-
truders are assembled like moviegoers
with Roman noses. When we hide behind
snow chains, the farandole dies quietly.

6

In the bleachers we sit watching the buhl
around their complexion become dark like
dulcamara. Fascism is hit-and-run
beyond historical materialism
and the imaginary republics
of khaki and locomotives. Rude boy,
put away your comae of bush tele-
graph, the sheepdogs are here, and their athlete
lumberers. Many trees will be felled. Many
replicas will find their true street value.

7

I come to Truffaut's aesthetics with a
boatload of fosterlings. Adoption is
not my game, under anybody's flag
of convenience. Egress is by way of
the blue eiderdown, the vulture's fin-de-
siècle seclusion. We feel alone
when not alone, we dive into sulfur
in a sodden trailer-park mode: voix cel-
este, well-tempered old world, insectarium
around the flame tree, brisket of brilliance.

8

The music we sightsee today, amidst
the thousand and one nights' thought disorder,
is demilitarized. The maps drawn by
chihuahuas are little boo-boos you must
ignore. You could read the Anschluss, or an-
orexia, it would be the same, the af-
ternoon is a faithless lover. Fairy
ring, you circle my melodica in
desire born of burning glass, though I have
not yet paid off the franchise's bad debt.

9

It is ridiculous when we ride the
cymbals whose shellwork liberates us toward
the correct hemisphere. I rotate the sun
as a hausfrau is religious, stone dead
in the conservatory, a house of glass
consequential to no dragonflies. Are you
up to your elbows in your great sense of
humor? What is the human interest
here? Who is Humpty Dumpty? Can we pad-
lock our canoes before the rags of dawn?

10

They came with reams of reportage, which sound-
ed good to my trained ears. They claimed the station
house was on fire. Someone's stature needs a
peg down, a candid body press. I have
not said your chaconne deliberations
put a dent in my clerical collar.
Only that your letter of intent always
arrives on time, catches me in the midst
of mouthwatering ragas. This is a
no-go area, this paean to kneeling monkeys.

11

I wake up to perceive your deciduous
shedding: Paul Bowles said it well in *The Shel-*
tering Sky. (It is a boyar's last privilege.)
Grandmother clock whose hyperextension
is a landslide in time, mermaid's purses
hiding behind coal scuttles left from a
past century, images of merlins
and ronins as hardened as flag-flying:
all the ghost paraphernalia of a life
well-lived, stretched like a flamingo's long neck.

12

Flamethrower! Nazi! Indiscreet questioner!
What happened to the star-spangled banner,
the hidden agendas of excretion,
Orpheus in his disorderly house, da
Vinci's first-day cover, imaginary
report cards to sand fleas, counting sheep to
sleep? I know what happened. At 45
rpm the formalities stick, but
the troposphere can handle only so much
exaggeration before it forgets.

13

Dear forkball, hello! And also the silence
of interlard. Let us walk across the
mantletree and detect cat footprints, par-
allax sight rhymes. I was almost forced to
learn stenography, would you believe it?
I have faith in the third-person point of
view, it usually yields more employment,
it is a way around the broken chords
of angel-dust shame. I am on the side of
cephalic baptisteries, the names for daylight.

14

What is the darkness of carabineers?
I see on the hilly path toward the dis-
cus many strands of herringbone mantras,
I hear them in the montages of deictic
congeniality. Spit out the dottle:
the intaglio of 19th-c. sickness
is an imperial feint, despite Jesuitical
faith. I am jealous of hooligans, the bru-
tality of granaries, warm fuzzy
writing without the hope of self-repair.

15

The bridge passage was cathartic in an
understated way. Embowered in fab-
ulism, draped in gingham curtains of oaths,
I failed to be a modernist. Or at least
a rectilinear one, a supremacist
of small candlelight. It is not up to
us to lower our voices against the
brawny cracker-barrel mouth of fascism.
Ghostly is the moth, ghostly is the town,
the harvest moon can be seen jumping off.

16

I drank lapsang souchong (the sound of it),
reading one by one the blockbusters of
liturgical neuroses, and suddenly
media studies emerged in Moravia,
mystagogues who spoke of Lacanian stages
of grief (or language or harangue or shock),
and my happy hour was over. It
was over in a leap second, before
I could contemplate a second strike. Nor
did my shape memory ever recover.

17

I went to Shangri-La in 1933.
There were speaking trumpets on the roads which
you described thus: "Moonflowers are moody.
The digraph is a faulty ligature.
Between your Aramaic cuisine and my
bargeboard is a confessional." The monks
of Hecate were Good Samaritans, all,
tactful like thimblefuls of brandy. Ty-
phoons that year (born Samuel Rosenstock)
came to the verge of tears, my last white night.

18

They met at Dumbarton Oaks in the era
of rugged union players: Muriel Rukeyser
was in decline, and neuropharmacology
was never-ending. Upon failing to
kill the sphinx I suffocated my
uterine klan (or Klan), and there we stood,
watching the hanging baskets all come down,
loaded with cannabis. It was a time
of secret cancellations, allemande
dancing, building post-and-beam security.

19

The evidence is tamper-proof. That you
like the chaste tree's corrugated itch, that
you loosen the notations in the mar-
gins of the sabbatical year: every
turkey shoot comes with its own style of ear-
phones. To deify you is to accept
fertility, which I do. We play court
tennis come what may, on Monday mornings
in chlorite, in our granular fantasyland.
Industrial parks are in the future still!

20

To be a poet (Indy car) of radium
emanation or stoop labor or contract
bridge: what is associative memory?
Items are identified by content,
not address, which is to say there is al-
ways a skeletal reminder of the
celestial pole. Standing over you (berg-
amot orange), watching your allegories,
I am torn about the lengths to which I
can go to announce the jump shift I stole.

21

Dear jungle cat! Or what others have called
error correction (we are all in error
until time is called, until the Council
of Chalcedon goes to war over its
own body), or knowing cannabis by its
true name: belles-lettres is arduous, because
we bellow like alcoholics, we are
absent among the craftswomen, and the
shooting script is not a list, not a trolley,
not the deadstick landing of feline hope.

22

I talk about crystal glass a lot. Every
morning balmy class consciousness visits
my hair space. Then you start your monologue:
"Seasonal affective disorder. Oh yes,
the Colosseum and its salt chuck. I
will dig my talons into dhobi itch,
or dhikr, or diabolism. En famille,
we go out to the ancient of days. Hippie,
do not lactate! The spider is my corposant.
We are unisexual? Or uninhabited."

23

Midships, the shoulder holster fell off, I
stood on the deck and composed a short story:
tobacco plants, vigilance committees,
coronary thrombosis, what they used
to call the dispossessed of the earth, these
all featured prominently. What is in
dispute is genealogical fide-
lity: I am my father's sole halyard,
waving to the seas, a magus owning
rejection slips, relaxed in your ripples.

24

I read myself the riot act. How sweet
it was to make of the frontispiece a
road to exclosure. Child of the seventies,
exonerate the faithful, they have been
falconers producing the Indian burn.
I am indisposed, referred again, un-
happy. The poets are on the same wavelength,
somewhere between desire and descent,
featherweights knowing plenty of foreplay.
The gendarmerie marches to syllabics.

25

Sufism leads to the synod of jo-
joba and an inch of mercury: I
have indulged all too much on the green earth,
have been a rumormonger, though the news
is in the end transparent. You must be
a plant in the transit lounge to know about
being buck naked for the sake of fa-
mily medicine. Every child is a
hedge against improbity. Every kid
brother turns out lonesome like Mach numbers.

26

Patient Lucy, you are Shirley MacLaine
in a macintosh, postmodern patriarch
for the rebroadcast (ray florets sequestered
for the right serenade): yes, sordino
suits the sorcerers, they kill tanagers
with sobriety, they stand at the trailhead
inviting us to walk the path, littered
with tractarianism. The vestibule
has a beam compass, borrowed for the day:
competence matters, dramatic erections.

27

What is equitable in the age of grief?
I present my felix culpa to the
assembled hawks, and they do not
have Hitler moustaches, none that I can
see. What comes out of it is impunity.
An itinerary for the juenesse dorée,
six or more parallel versions, the organ-
ization of satsangs for the crakes.
My sadness is deadwood. The day school is
just the gestation for higher animals.

28

I wrote a book about death but it had
everything to do with aesthetics: and
what does *that* mean? Is it how I wield the
pooper-scooper amidst the religious
poplars? How I remake the stem christie
for the thigh-high stepbrother? Words are thin,
words are ventilatory, words are blue-
bonnets incapable of blunder. Antares
falls in my lap after advanced placement,
we were not adulterous in Bryce Canyon.

29

I am stretched like Brunelleschi among
temporary supports: the brusque sky in its
Brythonic moments is an ode to formal-
ism: I would always bet on the red fox,
the picaroon to ascend the sterling
stepladder, and toadflax to breed as natural
as weeds. I have never owned a home in my life:
and did you ever hear about the children's
crusade? There actually was one, in 1212,
of which poetry has no known record.

30

There is laughter about "sadomasochism."
Uncomfortable laughter. Carving-knife laughter.
There is an aqueduct that runs through the
middle of the brain, much as you think of Er-
ebus, son of chaos. The equipage
is spiral and distant and finite, to
hang you mercifully. Ismail Merchant
should have stopped at *Shakespeare Wallah*? But he
was the mother hen in the spark chamber,
he lit up the hambones in grammar school.

31

I am old as Mohenjo-Daro. Tough mo-
hair draping my desert incontinence,
as I search for (white) theurgy in ordinary
signs: such as chlorella turning greener and
greener despite the acidic sun, fossils
you would expect to be disgraced by disease
going on and on in forethought, the smell of
Oman drifting to the paddling pool (olivine
pages not yet written for lack of a script),
letting the eagle owl go, letting him live.

32

How deep is the earth almond buried? Ex-
cavations have proceeded apace since the
fracturing of colonialism. There is
a bit of a goth in all of us who
avoided internment. What is court dress?
What is courage in both hands? My cousin,
mummery you will find on every seesaw
in every land, and also separatism
without cause. Do not be seduced. The seraphs
are light and ardor only in the thickets.

33

Our ears are thick on the ground (touch-me-not!),
vitalism, or folk medicine, or
drinking songs, all of it drizzling upon
my consort. Did we play the cittern? Did
the blintz satisfy you? The food was like
the infant bambino, infant among
infants, amusing like the amulets
we took so seriously. You were amorous
by the culvert (eyes like Depression glass),
the historic present in the great food chain.

34

Historically, Rousseau is the model
for the hundred flowers to bloom, or not, hurrah
anyway! The husk of individuality,
jinn and lechery and lebensraum and leatherwear,
he said it all before the fact, and we have
rabbit fever still. The tour d'horizon
was meant for draft dodgers and bioscientists alike,
it's not as if the angelica trees survived
the Battle of Passchendaele. You scratch my back,
and we meet the sculptor in his temple.

35

We meet the tenderhearted uninvoked
in eras of wee-wee weeping: the woodlands
are drab-colored, the carving of xylog-
raphy is grumpy, the yajna on the
yacht is all foam and wounds. Nostalgia
is always at someone else's expense,
like a savvy graphic novelist with an
expense account. In Tampa Bay, so much
crying, likewise at the Catawba River,
and all the talk is of fireless cookers.

36

What is your favorite triangle? Do you
have one? I am partial to…the secret
police bothers me again, in my second
childhood. Will you undress me? I hear vox
angelica in Foucault's abnormal-
ities, and when I look through the Dobso-
nian telescope. Please hold the cue cards right.
I get the collywobbles whenever
you show me your catalog and cast my
bread upon king penguins and serranids.

37

If I touched you, I thought I was touching
a stone, or rather a glaucophane dance:
on Lombard Street we are lonesome and mad,
the mother figures cannot get into
the mosque, we cannot touch the search coil. Son,
Stella Maris watches over you when
you cry in your sleep, the Chassidim have
the blue flu, don't you know it? Science is
androcentric, but art and war live out in
the consumer society as mellophones.

38

One of the three magi, me in the mega-
store, sloshy, subdivided, stoic. Oscar
Wilde is timeless, so are Proust and James, they
were texture mappers for tête-bêche after-
noons when it seemed like you could live on croc-
odile tears alone. How do you make time stop?
Do you condone the barbarism of chalk
talk? Humanism came of age with bulk mail,
went out of style with bullet points. Please, Meph-
istopheles, monotypes are necessary.

39

Rain tree, a show for percussion, sorcer-
ous vanilla dress distracting me from the
real cortex: the mind is a costar with
divisions of the divining rod, catch-
ing me flat-footed every time. They do
not roll out the red carpet for me ever
since I redeemed myself with title deeds.
Time is unconsidered, uncompetitive,
uncomplaining, while we utter honest-
to-goodness definitions of chintz.

40

Where does the sand collect? In the regions
of the mind where botany is chipping
away at the awkward age (of least motion),
the dead man's fingers are always
playing: a music of forked lightning, gluti-
nous historiography, the hive vibrating
to the mummy's notepaper. The silhouette
inspiring spin-the-bottle is slow torture
compared to the way the lazars escape
with lead in their arms and row the boats.

41

When you gloss upon my laws of gloves and
worms, I am no longer the first primate:
it is a sect of aqueous humor we
follow, being in love with the touch of bag-
pipes. I will go to Asimov's Russia
tomorrow seeking trouble. The American
dream lives on in acid house, at its
bedside the Dewey system reaches 999,
and the Equality State is where we all
live. Is this epiphany even-handed?

42

I gave up evil to please the featherbrains.
Together we grangerize books given to
grand apartheid, inserting javelinas
and lizardfish. How do we metabo-
lize the oversampling from centuries
of scroll bars? To burn a library is the
sound shift we sometimes need. No, I
don't mean that. Theory says that capital
goods are everlasting. I cannot be Charon
anymore than you can be a distich.

43

The distant early warning says that we
are homogenized into equal parts nec-
tar and guns. Will you be parsimonious
for my sake alone? I wandered inside par-
quetry. There I heard paronyms that boiled
down to this signal: "Cut glass is divulged.
The existential quantifier fools no one
in the age of frankness. Do not hitchhike.
Take me to Lloyd's Register to find mal-
feasance. You can keep all the mandalas."

44

Orwell lived in Mandalay and so did I,
we were punched in the face, reduced to pulp-
wood, made to wear tea gowns: the police
not yet techies, their wingspans from the
dark ages, their basal ganglia not yet
bowing and scraping. Still we found solace
in the choo-choo train, speeding past our
coprolite imaginations, full of Galen's
methods, Hellenic improbabilities.
The Java Sea ran deep like alien guilt.

45

To be irreparably alone in the
guest house you devised from the magnetic
moment: it is all I can do to restore
my resting potential, jack no one around,
escape the identification parade.
What is your involvement with the world of
objects? Do they seem to you heli-skiing
while we are acting out the jailbreak?
What makes the silence of objects leakproof?
(Objects are lamentations of fortune.)

46

I have not yet formulated gold, nor have I
experienced goggle-eyed inhibitions:
this one was a lulu, this Luddite killed
by the minutiae of the minyan: there
were too many, too many I saw in the
mirror, too many per capita, ref-
ugees from Delilah. Formalism
means to forgo homocentricity,
to relive the Iron Age on the Irra-
waddy: insolvent, insomniac, imperial.

47

What is implanted in my mind when I
travel through the Imperial Valley? Of course
Old Norse and its rhythms, but perhaps also
some of O'Keeffe's sculptures of scur-
vy. And perhaps I am thin in the cirro-
stratus, though the civil death (at the bottle
tree) remains benign. You speak to me of
Andalus again as though bragging rights
were something to cultivate. The culture
we have known is one of folie à deux.

48

Mathematically, it is impos-
sible: to outpace Malthus, to calculate
the sucking louse, to fortify eloquence.
Yet we try. Poetry is something of an
ellipsis: it is the quiet enumeration
of foundries that turned to dust, old dead gut-
tural languages spoken in kasbahs,
men-at-arms who died on Nazarene roads
ill-equipped for opening nights. The unclimb-
able spider's web is a jingle shell.

49

The hyssop I sprinkled over iambus
(*Doctor Sax* and *Big Sur*), giving my side
of the story to the lead article:
the leviathan is ear-splittingly close,
but I know how countertransference works.
Your constatives are rare and celulloid
fractions: they add up to the fragrance of
the geometer moth. Inside the mollusk
lives the opera queen, his orderly room,
the ramada where papillons obsess.

50

I learned about Occam's razor early
on, and took it to heart, and still do. What
is obvious is that the referendum
will never occur. The reflex arc of ro-
manticists is at root a hold button:
we cannot get past the Good News Bible,
we cannot be captains of the Flying
Dutchman. The harlequin stands mute, not yet
inhumed, not yet jumbie bird: my medina
the hobo jungle, hard partizan camp.

51

Dear biographee! Sit tight by the scrolling
amnion while your arabesque biopsy
unfolds: it is not fair to call your in-
vocation a fantasy. Everything
hinges on the gazette coming through, lapses
in macaronic confessions notwith-
standing. What is the true lyric position?
Can it be loud? The noumenon that is
pace notes comes once in an adventurer's
life: I do not believe in abreaction.

52

If I told you I was an absentee
landlord you wouldn't believe me, just as
you would laugh at my editorship of
fatwas on Juno. What happens to local
color at the Niagara Falls or in
the Rust Belt? Is sterilization ever
ethical? Is thanatology or
imperfect competition or the hen-
house? From Wallace Stevens I learned grounding:
how enthalpy is the soul of dismis-
siveness, and not to fear the boubou's call.

53

Catamite that I am, the French twist defines
me, likewise halophile individuality:
the lutenists have left the city, left it
to the lunatic fringe, the nighthawk and
the palace coup. I won consistently
at cribbage: this too is a lost gener-
ation. In the palaestra candleberry
boys divide before our eyes, like heat death.
The safest caste is bhang, just enough
colostrum, fabulous color-blindness.

54

The incompleteness theorem states that of
all the private keys only the resur-
rection plant survives, that the booby prize
is carnal knowledge, that follicles are
either full-length or gargoyle-sounding.
There is much that poetry, growing out of
the rent-free mimeograph, cannot handle:
this is not a sorrowful statement. Stylops
have a busy pawnbroker life, growing
into epiphora, into latex knife-pleats.

55

They landed at Douala, a little dotty,
gender-neutral, great attractors, light-footed,
initiating the pageant of spectator
time counted in sweetheart roses. In the
traffic circle effeminate diacritics
inquired about known degrees of freedom: the
answer was always in the box pew (catenated
and biting), as authentic as bitterroot
for allomorphs. Language, accelerated,
is the last clink heard before clinical death.

56

It is impossible to be consistent
over the duration of the glimmering.
Pearly gates are dedicated to rainmakers
and secondary colors: the world awakens
each morning to bibliomancy. In the
ashrams (of annual rings) nothing but cap-
ital punishment, nothing but twinging
dharma. To create the perfect halftone
illustration it helps to have seen the
oilfields fighting the twilight of the gods.

57

The moon blooms in occupied hours: what does
my sixth sense tell me about my honest
métier, how will the nation treat me? The
object-world is obscene not just to me, but
to the roundheads on the sidelines. Phrygian cap
I wore in times of tantric strangulation
freed me for a moment, yes, but in the
end the strawflowers and honey mushrooms got
away from me. I feel the earthquake. The
field hospital is leveled to the ground state.

58

A gazelle comes to me in my dreams. Jap-
anese paper I carved under the maypole:
pilot of the pillowcase, pill popper,
radioman, secessionist. I slept through
the slave trade, a willing tenant at will.
Chilblains grow during consciousness-raising
in the fixer-upper, the five pillars
of Islam are as dated as the hit
parade. Dear kibbutznik, there are lawbreakers
amongst you, teach them natural history.

59

The history of poetry begins with a
national convention at which pump jockeys
were sprinkled over with sprigs of temer-
ity. At first they liked the Turkish baths.
And also hibernation (the living
death) on the paddleboat, knowing nothing
of the primal scene. Then the spirograph
recorded tropes of voyeurism (Walter
Mitty) fed by the wardrobe mistress. It
didn't take long to excel on Walpurgisnacht.

60

My novel has been excerpted by an
entity whose exact glossary has been
hijacked. At high noon I walked into the
Hejaz in a paddy wagon, viewing through
the rangefinder my readers who partook
of rasas in raw sienna. I was
blinded by the signatories, whose sole
purpose, it seemed, was to dissolve me in
tartaric acid. In none of my stories
will you find unadulterated trousseaus.

61

Freedom, for the victors over Vivaldi
(bad Vikings, distracted by ditchwater),
means nothing so much as a living flight
recorder, the Hebrew Bible performed
by Ben Hecht and the heckelphone, hedges
against the microclimate in neo-
liberal rooms of palpitations (palm wine!)
and road maps. You are lying to me (slip-joint
pliers over my sloshy mouth), but I
let you, I play your angry slot machines.

62

In the stovehouse svelte plants (shaped to
farthingales) whose farmhouse beauty
is nothing like classical statuary:
trotting toward the Tropic of Cancer I
met flammable owls and galliwasps, all
the tropes of Munchausen's syndrome. You take
care of me in the multiverse (and the
multiversity), my trophic schlock, my
pretense to textbook Sherlock. You produce
the wah-wah effect every long weekend.

63

At the weigh station, they found I had lived
behind a window of half-integers:
daddy to whatever speaks on behalf of
hashish, camerawoman whose etiquette
knows nothing of ethnology. The Sho-
shone have a name for shrinking violets
(pagan biostatistics), behind the bamboo
curtain the counterinsurgency looks
for its estrous cycle, and the hyperdrive is
as near as mannequins in mousseline.

64

Please come to my moveable feast. It hap-
pens every time the Götterdämmerung
takes a break from Newton's laws of motion,
it happens whenever my tranquil war
fits well with the Sanhedrin I have built
from the paperwork of sufism (I mean
what remains suffocated in the ther-
mostat): ask the turkey vulture to cough,
cough so hard the brick veneer falls off, as
does the gossip column on the futon.

65

It is the gospel truth, that Gorky (Arsh-
ile) knew in his own lower depths: that the
iron horse was invented to carry
untruths across the opera-glass landscape
not only faster but like a spendthrift's
last extravaganza. I think of pea-
cock blue in my ore (my core of pecu-
liarities) as something like pearlware,
to be flaunted and grumbled about. No to
the new look (calf-length skirts) and junk oboes.

66

The old believers pile on, try to recruit
me into their quinquennial rapprochement
(quidnuncs all): Oppen, Zukofsky, Olson,
Mandelstam, Lorca, Apollinaire, Bataille,
Breton, all of them rappelling down the
bold steep face of repopulation. The
world as we know it now (not the one from
church planting) is a nude cinematic
cancelbot: you are only to have a thought
if you break it down in gutbucket solos.

67

I once knew a guniter who was gung-ho
for the single-lens reflex: his stationary
state was fireblight, the episcopacy of
the dismal swamp. He would have disinher-
ited me of my pilgrimage to Broken
Arrow, which I had planned on for years
before the beat frequency became something
for antiquarians to play with. I am
not anybody's antitype, least of all
the smiling hagiographers of the poets.

68

The laws of war are clear: you do not give
in to morganatic parsimony,
you do not act like a card shark at the
box social. Charity (elbow room) in
your gaze, medusa that is off-limits
to a studious shepherd like me, spring fever
on the tarmac, the task (Tyrian purple) all
too typhoidal. I am useless among
aquiline antonyms, they make me faithful
to the ice age brushing over the hill station.

69

Middle school (Jemez Mountains) je ne sais
quoi, fraternizing with the Jesse tree,
all the cousins-german (cowabunga!) on the
carrot-and-stick carousel: without straw,
without bricks, without the Archimedean
screw, every arcade is uncovered, bare of
Orphism. The lyrical use of Orthodox Judaism
(why not?), the sporangium colors bursting
out of timeshifts: vaccinations work even on
the wealthy, even on the weak-minded.

70

I write a poetry of detachment. Li Po
once loved the flowers of confederacy
like a man in detention. How can I
be free of dramatic irony? The glass
lizard appears out of nowhere, when I ask
indirect questions of the horoscope.
The moon has the last word. I took the narrow-
boat and headed for the redbuds, with me
a symphonic poem (becoming a com-
mon prayer): fade-in, fade-out, and then landfall.

71

If I had a blue guitar, with the air
of a destroyer, what would the mea culpa
amount to? The mean sun moves through these streets,
like spitchcock sliding out of grasp. At night
trick cyclists charge the half-bloods of causing
too much stress amongst the body politic.
I digress. Lolita grabbed a longbow
and aimed it straight at the heart of motion
sickness. The mother country is a Ouija
board lit up by shelterwood paralogisms.

72

Early in the morning, dressed in a sher-
wani gifted by tangerine relatives
(unionists all), I considered volun-
teerism. A weanling still, my time (after
the wedding night) has been a mortise lock,
broken only by morphic resonance.
If I wake up in Morocco, I go
to sleep in Gran Canaria. The head-
master had a note for me: wipe out the
graffiti, today the lord mayor should visit.

73

Then we went to learn to be mahdis.
We ate the maguey plant, built picture palaces,
followed the rural route, lived at the skating
rink, owned that the ghats needed to be cleaned.
The ghost in the machine is not what you think.
The solution is always cortisone,
say the chemists of distance learning, the
time for galactagogues was at birth. Now
you are old, your skin is gorse, and larceny
will land you in Kaliningrad (ice-free!).

74

To accumulate (via glassblowing)
a fungiform congregation, delighting
in one's cellular wit, the home videos
dedicated to homoousian melodrama:
this only adds to the melancholy,
the slow death of the rose quartz and its sight
gags. Yes, it's funny how your conspectus
excludes so little, how it is a blurb
that never blushes. The end comes too soon, like
Aubrey's *Brief Lives*, or the century plant.

75

There is a reason the cerebrum is
divided into two parts: Europa,
moon to dark lines, incarnation of the
left brain, is likewise mobile to those given
to naches. The nagas are part rapparrees,
part sign language, but I understand only
the formal silkscreen. We are all gods, or
coruscating birds, falcons who run out
of finitude. The air of this fine print
cannot break through the nestled integument.

76

You see, poetry does criticize itself
(and if the novel is dead it seems likely
to me that people just can't bear narrative):
said Oppen. And I think too that the mind
is by nature Nestorian, or rather the readership
of posterity (for which I write), nepo-
tism reeking through their every pore: the rank
and file have honor societies to get
past, which they can't, because time can only
be frittered, it is not slow-melting tallow.

77

Your ginseng death comes as news to me. I
stand advancing maxims and homeschooling
for my nieces and nephews, Mayans next
of kin to me only in the sense of
dull reportage. The ripple in Tabriz is
heard far off. I am unconsummated,
accepting the costermonger's compliments,
feeling ergonomic. Gracioso, they
call me in error: massa, massa, the
shock workers beat again the talking drums!

78

Some morning, take the time to observe
the takin (deep in the Himalayas) pursue
its hunt: it takes something back, or it takes
nothing back, just as vin ordinaire tastes
extraordinary depending on the
idée fixe for the day. Take the time to
teach the hired hands something of Horowitz's
impressions, something of the orphanage
Ortega y Gasset and Horkheimer
left behind to damn the short story's temper.

79

I do shoulder stands. You watch from the safety
of the stellar wind, questioning my flip-
pant focal point. All I have to say is:
"the cold wife lay with her husband after
her death," and then to add, "except God, who
seems a nuisance from the point of view of
Key West." These are all facts well-known: that *The
Decameron* is not yet finished, the
loving cup is empty, empty, and the view
from the mirador is one of simoleons.

80

At the botanical gardens, we take
the blue devil under the capitulary
(not so secret), as demonology,
for once, is not ivory black, not kruger-
rands, but marrowbone that plays on nativism.
Not a stickler for reported speech, you
repel thigmotropism: everything
moves in reaction, like a corsage in
wind, like the carnival breaking free of
the black swan. Such a loud amen corner!

81

After the end of justice (in Nicaragua
endless nights of ngoma), transposed from one
continent to another, one century
to another, the reed pipe still sounds the same.
Some believe in satanism, some think
Paul Theroux wrote of actual places, some
are ennobled by flamethrowers. Etesian winds
cause a sense of literatim to take hold,
we become new age imitators of
medical degrees, meeting in the middle C.

82

And how do you sleep? At midweek the rep-
rimand was issued and it took me a
while to shiver. I'm still looking for the
swimming hole we loved so as children. The
easterly direction I have lately
taken follows nothing but the contour map.
The braziers caught fire, then the command
post, then the foundries of Hippocratic
oaths: I wrote many drafts of "intrusion,"
knocked about by the minstrel show's minus signs.

83

Before I knew it, the Egypt of my
epyllion dreams vanished in a puff of
Freemasonry: I was grasping for habitable
corners after I finished with lower
criticism, hiding the moonstone at
the open mike. The plan is to overissue,
overgrow, overgraze, let the phallus
not be pettifogged into purity.
Relativism, in rhetoric, is forgivable,
the ruth I feel at the death of the saber-
toothed tiger is not the scutwork I do.

84

Magicians, silo-haunted, carrying
signboards of toad-in-the-hole pessimism,
let the kids taste tutti-frutti in the
bazaars of the Khmer: you are not invited,
nor is your library science, it doesn't
work where the locksmiths (of madrassas) refuse
to be meddlesome. Meow, and meow again!
Take all the morphine you need. Here are your
characters for opera buffa, all around
you, staring in astonishment at the
Order of the Garter, flexing pectorals.

85

I follow the pearly eye around the
fields of Ponca City, the butterfly
enacting the Greek cross in hindsight. The
fields are in a state of hyperbole,
inundated by liriodendrons and
Osage orange, the night journey has for
once become panic-stricken. Pantagruel-
ian banquet (quick quick breath!) requires a
quorum of the sitting dead, so we
decide to press the mute button (and narrate).

86

The story is this: in the rucksack I steal,
I find sago pudding, and a sheath for
your dabbling duck. You take off to Dada,
leaving me czar of crépinettes, inviting
my crab-necked friends for some mild-mannered
conservancy. Then your carriage is
assaulted. They are brazen, the thieves, de-
manding, on the spot, fake genealogies
of the gods. When I rescue you, you are
inhibited for life, but a touch lactescent.

87

Poetry is labor-intensive. Summon
the lonesome Makhpiya-luta, the scriptures
of Maimonides, the military band
(migraine, migraine!), then you'll have the sweet myrrh
(penmanship) that comes from Rainy River:
penetralia you must enter with every
arm of yours (or Neil Sedaka's) in sepsis.
Poetry is parenthesis, the diplo-
matic pouch in which you hide dirhams, cotton
rats, the Little Dipper, the Maxim gun.

88

Speed, the great futurist illusion, to which
I sacrificed metempsychosis: I knew
there was something to it, but I wanted
to rush orphan drugs to market, and my
peach fuzz became a rainbow beard overnight.
Ragtime, your moment will not recur, your
enthusiasm was like fast-talk on top of
collective memory. We cannot remember
the past, we cannot benefit from it,
as long as the funnel cloud twists and twists.

89

The human life we love most arrives
again as bird of prey (enlightened), the
cold unseeing eyes enormous and fer-
mented: they see gerontocracy as
the last chapter in iconoclasm
(frustules of luminescent strife), as the
young get old by the minute, hair grows gray,
and the luna moth I spoke of years ago
turns into lynx-eyed mukhtar: governing
us through primary (ocelot) colors.

90

I see the ghost of my ginger cat running
through the house, a shadow of an ice-cold
shadow, vanishing before I get a
good look, just as it was in life. Did I ever
touch you through your hardworking (grueling) heart?
At the patent office devices have been
registered in the name of patria, but
they no longer believe the rest cure helps.
In the shade sightlessness, in the mirror deform-
ity, because grace cannot be directly touched.

91

To get the story out before deindus-
trialization builds pace, and the
cinematized factories of my childhood
give way to the circus of birdwatching
and apple-cheeked applause: do you see how
commodification makes us fall in love
with the eugenics of euphoria? At times
I was fratricidal, for reasons of state.
I mentioned the Frankfurt School before, grue-
some herrenvolk looking down on hosteling.

92

It may be that I hide (intrapreneur
or poet, writing in vacuo glosses), be-
hind curtains of kudzu, so prolific
it would take a Kurosawa to stop it.
It may be that I lock out faint lobelia
images: too pretty, like dying narwhal.
No one stops me. Stop me, before my pud-
ding face enters a state of rapture with
he who stopped writing at twenty, because
the third eye is always touch-and-go.

93

Take a deep breath. Watch the touchscreen turn to
the turquoise of your dreams. The vase shell is
a predator too (the word of the century),
what is left in the washtub when you are
done with me are a bow of sugarcane,
a bowstring of bees, and arrows of flowers.
Was the Kaleyard school right after all? If
I skipped kindergarten, it was a low-key
fact. Every morning I wake up to the
same old mandamus, drowning in marsh gas.

94

Yes I said death is a festival, but that
was by way of definition: every
word you learn is a matchboard of possi-
bilities, a nautical mile you travel
at your peril. I did not mean cele-
brations, like parrot fever, or Parnell's
obstructive tactics. In the summer, sitting
by the pitahaya, dead or pistol-whipped,
we recall hide-and-seek on the Silk Road,
when we each had a rumored fatal flaw.

95

This is hand-to-hand combat, this wrestling
between the (failed) jazzbo and his several
admirers: in the mirrors in the bathrooms
in the French Quarter the lemurs have their
way with licorice (despite malocclusion),
they lick the unwrapped mummies like pagan
dark chocolate. So much spare chromium
energy, so many ways to campaign
against indirect rule, so many karateka
putting on the loincloth to play the marimba.

96

"My dear Joyce, there are two things about you
which are unchangeable": and I too have
had many childhoods, one after the other,
not the kindness of the destroying angel,
but living in a hyphenated frater-
nity of jealousies known since Mordred,
building the mood for moral rearmament.
It has been revealed at last that no one knows
me ("a way a lone a last a love a long"),
but don't be old, don't be sad, don't be ill.

97

You wrote chapbooks. "Party referred to...
brilliant capable man but had unfortunate
start." As to Faulkner, who has seen the un-
written corrigenda? Not the enlisted
men, not the evil interrupters, not
the lost tribes. They grow mossbacked in their moth-
proof retirement homes, fondling the sweetheart
necklines as though for the first time, shunning
eidetic images for abstractions
smelling like demented Egyptian plovers.

98

The Chinese have a wonderful term, wei chi,
when it comes to animal rights (as long
as I can remember I kept snakes, turtles,
insects, pigeons, parrots, fish): and wrote novels
by the Feldenkrais method. This looks like
government-issue hypercorrection,
they do it now to the leonine cities
their mythomania (faulty retinitis)
bills as real cities: what is real about
the eccentric cities of ecology?

99

Nabokov knew nothing of ecossaise.
He stood astride the edifice of mel-
ancholia, sad as mordacious neoteny,
keeping neighborhood watch. Couples embrace,
then disengage, all the while not knowing
the rounds of silica gel in which they
have been encased. Behold the silk-cotton
tree, teacher of nativity. I put on
mascara (Klimt!), knit the Domesday Book, ad-
minister anesthesia to the mountain range.

100

At the end of quotations (rip-offs in
the nodules of outplacement) comes authen-
ticity—or what looks like a sheath knife
sticking into my ribs. It is all child's
play, a stylophone gifted by third parties
(unaccredited like the Turk's-cap lily),
turtledove calling and calling to you
as you extenuate. I have not ever
been cubiform, I am singing to you
of all the solo parts you have yet to accept.

Lyric/Resistance

Celan's interest in Yiddish usage also brought him up against the medieval roots of the German language. Like other twentieth-century poets, such as W. H. Auden or Francis Ponge, he must have been fascinated by dictionaries, especially etymological ones. What is certain is that he both loved and mistrusted words to a degree that has to do with his anomalous position as a poet born in a German-speaking enclave that had been destroyed by the Germans. His German could not and must not be the German of the destroyers. That is one reason why he had to make a new language for himself, a language at once probing and groping, critical and innovative; and why the richer his verbal and formal resources grew, the more strictly he confined them to the orbit of his most urgent concerns.

—Michael Hamburger, *Paul Celan: Poems* (New York: Persea Books, 1980), p. 20.

What is it to be poor,
I asked as a picklock.

The destitution of a
mauled corpse, wavering

in refinement, the pale
yellow fiber of an

echo's dismantlement.
Is it more than being

human? Is it less, when
you count the mail

and its expressions? It
came when I was looking,

though not in the way you
think, not in the base camp.

The bee. Its granola
fondness. The spark of
an orthodox saint

like me. The breath
of excretion, sodium and
splashed, unconsidered,

not talking, not talking
to willets. The curt buzz
of a onetime customer.

Above the operating table
stands a pathological surgeon,
whose path we illuminated

ten centuries ago: bathed in a cold
patois of Hashanah and blue
windows slavering over

hammers. The surgeon nods
to his attentive Sammys, who do
not want to touch his hands.

Buried deep in—the utility
of war, meaning how we were
colonials of furniture, washed
in birds, or at least I was—
given to studying antiques,
which felt to me after cookouts
like the gospel aftersound—of
war, whose apes, whose names,
whose steps we started with.

This body, like the corpus
of private law, takes a seat in
the proa, fluttering like

Sagittarius. Had I been
sterilized at an early age, I would
have had a conscious mind:

I mean, in the sense of
the tears of Job, who was in
league with conspicuous

writing.

The animals and I fail to come across in the leap year
and instead get caught up in reportage: who quashed whose
snubber with the clouds of Uncle Tom, whom we cut out
of the vigil of the staircase, whom we will argue our mental
states with. There are too many aspects to the unconscious
that Dada never captured, the animals say as they sink in the
Black River and take me with them to the dark blank eye.

My biggest fear is the rat.

Renoir, I mean Jean, is a scandal,
  when it comes to notation.

Observe the scapula.
It is often broken at the ebb.

I am ecology.
Possibly a fondler.

Of Jekyll and Hyde who was more likely
to order a mail-order bride?

A night monkey has patches of odeons and
stemma, when the egg splits open.

Through my shoulder blade an artistic
carving, exposing the mad matter of enlistment.

Of the malefactors who dress up corpses,
whom do you prefer to graze upon your navel?

A Nazarene the size of this building.
A skeptic who came through poison gas.

Day and night
I remember

the quality of
flash welding

which is the worm
coming home

to live among the
intoxicants.

When Christopher Columbus, disguised as me, sailed off…
Turn on the navigation lights, it is too dark for the relief map.
I hardly know when we have crossed from sea to land, or
if you'd rather, the soft rot that has set in my eyes. It takes
perhaps a decade or two before the way you groomed me,
upon the spiral track as a glass of wings, starts a deity.

The mind attends to a . . . towel perhaps.
Its two spheres are split, like Laurel and Hardy,

like the law according to parsimony.
When we watch the nations at war, we are

Madonnas depicted seated and drenched
in white wine. The mind hears a madrigal

and makes of it a passing bell, intent on
cultivating the sweetness of cabinetwork.

I would like to think that the mind pays tribute,
but we are vizards hidden in the firmament.

Some years ago
I wrote about dreams.

The first family,
satisfied with God,

and wanting
the narrator to rely

on parasites.
Some years ago I

ate up the subject
of dreams like tyranny

at very low frequency,
my true dialect.

The vast Indian subcontinent
is a diagram of layaway myths.

First, the resolution of the Miocene
age. Then minutiae. Varieties

of shirtsleeve fruit, the pink of
your tears, then teatime under trees.

They knew about tuning forks
a thousand years ago, in the age of

musk. In their medicine cabinets,
you find the hinges to mother's milk.

Paul Celan motivated me,
like externs on Libra, or perhaps

I am thinking of Philip K. Dick,
whom I have often mentioned,

in connection with the perceptions
of cars that don't cost a mint.

In the mirror the quillwork you
praised so highly really is static.

The mosque, interminate—
flattery's liturgic masque, where
we stand like problems,

but mellow,
melded to each other's surface oddities
in a packed assembly, shoulder
to shoulder, oily hearts
melting.

I buried, once, a porous sick distant uncle.
Or perhaps the uncle of an uncle. His holy relics
came in a remake of speakerphones, tar pits
of unwritten white paper. We raised our hands
to the ears, and paused, expectantly, as if
the silence of our pericardium would be jolted,
outmuscled, outperformed, by his little nest egg.

I will touch your nerve trunk,
said the teacher (Neanderthals, downfall,
rejection slip, reincarnation):

my relatives seeking medicine for transplanted eyes
and—oh, the teacher, I'm just spitballing a few

ideas over the open fire.
The sun, this morning over assembly, is a harvested
grapefruit I think I can touch, like a hobby.

The mantle
of a kerosene wick, dense engraving
above a fireplace: manners of scale, lighting, and perspective

in a classroom where music is never read.

Among the neopaganists, who all preferred
        a temperate climate, such as in Los Angeles before
the tanager's satin—but we dig in your satchel

        and find the exclamations of hoar!
You have aged anyway, those are the ground rules,
your skin, saline and vibrating, has turned into

  a baboon's silvery-gray cape and a naked red face.
Cutting their hamstrings, the neopaganists found that light
        curves in the lumberyard quite like child psychiatry.

Of the part that is Muslim in me (left
          behind by megaspores and subdivisions of class)
you know only the monotonous concentration.
A most respectable profession is body snatching.

 Bogtrotter, who loves vultures, repeats
to them, Let's hope, let's hope, let's hope...

Each language frames the same idea differently.
It's not just to do with words but the way agents are
executed after trial, phobias are flattened thousands
of times, the insupportable carries over into prophecy.

If you knew of my Khartoum insurrection...though I am
a glass jar with layers of pale foil on the outside, not
quite like a ski that has fallen off. In another language,
this would perhaps be incense that tears the heart muscle.

The pir hid behind a snowplow.
His weevil eyes, teal blue, Afghan,

truthful, as only cinerarium truths can
be. I saw Kabul snow behind circumcision,

I saw the circus in his reception room,
where acolytes bent and kissed his fat

palms, their hair smelling of detergent.
Snow fell like mist beyond open eyelets.

A quantity of ink
(in which I fell sick)

a record player
something fell in cascades

the tree that stood leaning
with its leathery fronds

the critical point of a frog
or a crow or a hero

children learn best by doing
moist cornered wings

Time,
invested in a section

of this book,
gnomon telling me

I could have been
highborn

behind the beam,
a knowing smile,

instead of strolling
in inferior courts

like a mandala
to wheelchairs.

These were known as dervishes
  (freshwater-lollipops, thick-skulled property),
vanguardists meeting in (lava) covens,
when not killing radio shows.

On the streets of the town (dead leaves
  and ripe fruit, abcissa/ordinate) we inhabit
through error, they amble (whirl!) past
our blemishes—fluid blennies, trim.

And to the point of the death camp, ask
  the dervishes what they think of air under
the wing while diving, how they divide
the book through grandmother's curtains.

Modern English has
  been around since about, oh, 1500.

The "r" pronounced in Britain
  is not the same as legal ownership.

It is something to reinvent the waltz.

Falling into liquid, the Dutch *spit*
  and German *spiess*.

The Secret Agent is interlanguage,
pidgin for facial collars, the least blurred

impression before art nouveau. The
predators of Yiddish hypnotize your

position of birth, until the mountain is
suitable for mining. But the second bomb…

My mother is gutty.
She is a trumpet to fasten on to
securely, she tells me
I'm her last-born child,
I will have the last word,
I will be the dead on Judgment Day,
I will lose the title to Li Po's light,
I will mime Rome and its stenciled copies,
I will mind the fire for finger-waggers.

I listen to her trumpet,
which blows open my kit bag,
and I go out in the world,
the tunnel of light dressing me,
nearer and nearer the date.

An open cluster of friends just like myself
on the playground of interviews,
everyday life as a genre (of Islam),
something that smells like paella in a large,
shallow pan,

the sea of hardwood trees,
a playground of fish natives and light balls,
hearing horses carrying loads of newspapers,
piercing holes in our little disorderly hands.

This brain,
a wooden or metal conduit
(handle with care, or Haydn go seek),
an Indian side dish of (home rule, government
by chasing rainbows)...the referees
are sick.

Milk and meat production,
placing the cross upside down,
sepulchral field of vision.

Ambrosial strawberry (bored a colony of
red deer):

                        in a hansom the schoolboys
prepare ready homonyms,
imagining a row of mummies
under a debt of

gratitude.

In Astoria, Queens, my checkbook—
  a chemistry of cordons,
  precious red fingers of a corpse—
bursts open. The deal we have made

            with dissolved air

is to read the north-wind-headlines,
  ask for climbing plants, open the air
  to leafletting. When you come in through
meaty land, I am your wire from the outside.

About three miles from your locked desk,
to worm-serving animal-density,
they speak of maya,
in the tone of housekeepers-turned-mothers,

            and I eavesdrop, with a long flattened tail,
motivated as the child of allusions.

What can they add to the conversation?

My grief, after all, is a male product,
formed by dehydrated tangerines and oranges,
as though bird excrement were gray metal,

            and I sit with you inside the parallelogram
            at intervals.

                                    Inside the tardy reply we sit in,
the sons of the previous king draw a pattern
of thin-filament trousers, move the horse
forward, denote the point on this particular
tropism, call a three-day truce, yet again.

Those who speak the language of maya—
            of truck gardens moving at moderate though certain
            pace, of parasites in a rout, of ten years of fire
            and waves of not playing hooky—
are like the children medieval poets gnawed on,
in the name of hormones,
as they worshiped the separate parts of each leg.

Moving along by myself,
on my own legs,
in the Truffaut-haunted tear-gas city,
I am wool, or imitation of it,
I kneel before the last of the Victorian houses,
I want the wheels that want greasing.

And following me, on their own two legs,
are the lieutenant dancers,
required by collectors of folk culture
to guard me in my mammal prison,
issuing warrants (like conductors' batons)
to prevent me from going to the beach
(picnic lunch at the cemetery).

Snowed in...
dear foxhole in the four-star city,

frambesia,
in the bricks-and-tiles encampment,
does not have the odor

of the neckline empire-builder.

There issued a long discussion among the magicians
assembled under the enchanter's nightshade. They were
the employees of Moors and the eighth-closest planet,
used to dogs with short legs and small ears, each with the
capacity of a bushel.

I knew them (burnsides and irrepressible
emotions) as records of the fossils spanning the length of
my short stories of loneliness.

Their tricks (of lava and
refractories and slag) gave me an income through painting
houses (in shades of anima).

Wear the apron, they order me!

At the delicatessen I see them playing tricks on the exiled
kings, their native countries, the dogs before breakfast,
all at once, as though their drab brown plumage were free.

It is the leap year again.
At the snowy park, I stumble
upon memento mori,
nude stockings
pointed in the right direction,
the ash of a person
who was a bore and a language
all unto himself.

These numbers are not
experimental errors. My classmates

are nubby, like new leaves,
like the wrong time of the evening.

Through (painted) oeils-de-boeuf
we can see in Harvard Yard

the old German composer, arisen
from his nearly dry oeuvre,

playing with the diseases of the teeth,
excluding the parent of the same sex.

Pamphlets rain down in the classroom.
Each of us imitates the bird's call,

pee-a-wee, pee-a-wee.

Some of them sell peyote buttons.
Their phantasmagoria include the practice
of religious aversion to the surrounding terrain.
I notice how they walk. They tell me they
are magnets. They come from Sinn Féin's
uneducated speech, and can often be mistaken
for important sex offenders. I wonder
at their slope-shouldered syntax, broken into
sterilized caviar and long, long muscles—
mastoids? I watch how they walk,
every stepfather thinking he is the years of a century,
every mother hidden above the waist level.

Thistle prickly thistle—
from earlier Utah,
some Marxist guerillas' tut-tut?—
come make white
lightning, the monks
have plenty to eat,
at the horsy
ash tree.

The old man—
caramel dipped in tutti—
maneuvering around predatory
ground beetles—
his eyes a caravan of trucks—
looking out over the sea
the vapor concurs—
to wear eyebright, marshy
flat-footed engines,
hijacked—
extremists plot his touristic demise—
the old man, logos of the one
index word.

I exercise my horse of classical music,
lighting the lamp along the edge of another
domino. The evening (maghrib) is a sea
journey centered on the midget submarine.

My friends of uranium burn me as a counter-
irritant, we talk about moving the piece on
the board game. I would not know the fresh
notes of bergamot for many more quatrains.

The crows scream—Holy Roman Emperor!
trawl net!—and the oud sounds from a close
distance, Osman, Osman, accept her offer,
sleep with her under the language of your people.

On the night before Eid,
in the bazaar of immortal horses,
we saw pewter spoons and knives
through which I wanted to wade.

The roundelay of bargaining,
coy simpatico flying aircraft,
exaggerated simper of brown pedals,
the new rupee of healing.

The alim held property as a tenant.
His language was earthquake. So, for example,
he told his followers that many an alternate
drama could be shaped to the solar plexus.

One among his listeners decided that the window locks
were useless. As someone with a pockmarked
face, he lived in outer space, as a lost planet.
A Nile crocodile was bound to carve up his desk.

What is the minimal pair?
Below the mother figure, below
even nursery rhymes and undergarments
and butterfly antennae?

In black-and-white spiral motifs
the language I was taught
in the plush chair time-out
sounds to me now as though it
is long slender leaves
missing the female parent.

The sick Muslims suffer from mosquito bites.
Before prayer, a smoke that repels new romantic music.
Female journalists form a nucleus of black shoes.
The bombs are timed to precision to let them catch up on their sleep.

Said the (witness of curatives) daughter
to her old mother, you resemble me in shape (female organs
of a flower), of a firearm power (well-shaft, stone-fruit,
stone of stones when urinating, and when not swaying
to the large hole in the ground), mother, she was saying, mother,
mother, mother (pitch bend), take me to the gaming tables,
the Provençal salt fish are ants, carpal bones in Roman provinces,
old age is but a graphic artist turned to the star Gamma Piscis Austrini,
mother, oh mother of slopes and roofs, teach me (pestle-uncertain)
the characters per inch the power of (hell) cylinders,
to use gold coins or not, to express as numbers the edible fruit,
or I might die as a small-amount rotor, my guitars might fail
(imitating alternating alternating sounds), apparently from (no stamens)
the long narrow canoes you did not give me, mother this is agriculture
(not pirated tapes), mother, when will you be born under the sun
in this sign, when will you rear and breed fish in casinos in charge of
gaming tables, fish that are like (urinating) words, I am the butt of your pistol,
I am the stone, the stone of a pair of fish tied together by our tails.

If this is a lament born of latex,
if this is an animal born bald,
if this is your white-crowned head,

then what about the silk thread of evil?

The children are streaked with red gemstones.
Getting blood out of a stone, out of a stone, blood, blood!

An animal's set of ancestors, getting ahead despite warnings.
The children are lizards that carry their heads in the raised position.

The rate of the heartbeat is drunk in blood, has red roots and leaves.
The city of hospitals is blockaded in two rows of blood feuds.

The ceremonial mingling of a woman and a woman's heart,
the parasite who lives in the aquarium, red-rhizome-aboriginal.

The children carry oxygen at a higher price, theirs is a drawing
held stationary, a drawing of combinations of centuries, sea-squirt.

For covering my eyelid with a neutral block of color (not black, not
black), the drop of liquid you see is paint, the block party's tissues.

The children of aquariums embark on retaliatory killings.
Their red gemstones arise from the color of our lipstick hair.

When you leave your (Egyptian black) country
your dreams change, they no longer (Let's hope so, eh!) have
weak teeth or sawlike projections.

Your dreams used to be what they call eidetic,
hieroglyphs of Sotheby's descent, egg-shaped cocoons,
unrestrained igneous-heartfelt effusions of trust.

Now your dreams are fruits flowing out of body cavities.
They are the effigies of the liquids of ovolo moldings.
You must swallow birds' eggs and every night spit them out.

Unemployed,
the northern sea duck
(Manhattan Beach-fake book)
passes through her faithless lover.

The falcon
in this fine and dry weather
settles on the fairway.

The grass is a grass of utopia.
The contemporary art fair
writes every week without fail.

The kids
don't get to watch TV on school nights.
The fairies are served with sour cream.

The most frightening dream—
Faisalabad, this restores one's faith (compass
to fake doctors): corresponding green.

The stalls and amusements for public entertainment.

Agriculture. Your pleasure, gladly, litigation-rugs.

The methods of our ancestors,
sickle-hooked northeastern Asia's small bright sky,
tiny like a proof,
the justice of snarling.

A rain, a crop,
a black silk dress with tiers of faggoting,
that the enemy may flee.

The. nerve of such a girl. when
regarded as a game. languages and other
indigenous languages and creole. in
medieval music. usually the third-brightest roof.
the female riding at. I don't want you
to know playful and. feminine of gamine. 1965, a
degree of risk, diplomacy a mature haploid-merry.
lead India out of poverty. G an octave.
ut indicating ut.

Who is clay mineral-illegitimate-dinosaur:
my daughter is seriously ill, horse-toothpower,
holly my relatives, my abdominal wall is illegible,

my scheme of meditations (from lava or magma),
who is Hector-killed lower body, iliac artery,
rolling infraorder, my holly is seriously ill.

Midweek, a heavyweight
throws rows of light at dunghill-panoramas

in an emotional crisis opened up by
popular song.

We are: linguistically Indian-paisa-oils-by-spraying.
Come mate, mate with turtle architecture.
Mate with Rahel, mate with the peace river, mate with
paying guests.

An article pawned, the fruit of this
neutrophil tree, many species of the pink of health, to which
the pineal eye adds a pinch of salt, when crushed, when crushed.

We will bury—
under musique concrète, processions
of the caricature of the normal self:

my wound that turns liquid
when the printer can't cope with
breath-text.

Cynosure of all eyes,
when you stepped into my do-si-do room,
I was no longer a grandson

of fruit in larval stages,
I was fuchsia feeling upset at costing
so little, I was a large gold refinery.

I arrived in London in a hackney carriage,
carrying in my pocket summers from Sudan,

knowing the Qur'an by heart, having created
a character named Hafiz, looking like a moor

in the harbor. The fishing, they said, since the
parole of the Western Atlantic, has been in a

state of complete happiness. The covert system
of trails (which leads to white wine) reinforces

the soles of my boots. I fish and I hunt and I
light the paths in crystals, I strengthen the enamel

of my hind limbs. A woman's stomach is a space
cut in the concept of innocence, which too has

received its fair share of narrative, the names of
buildings of counterintelligence. A small yellowish

limb playing at a computer terminal, I have started
being mentioned in indexes as the loss of information.

Patches of bright color—
    military action (no loss to the world),

the whole lot of them producing the knee of the foot
enabling the cardinals. My outer viscera,

    thoughtful shield,
hand-to-hand combat with adverbials,

drapery depicting the opening of the fireplace.
This is part of a writer's uniform.

Equivalent bones, whose metabolism
    of the prophet's stomach is minerals
    in a vertical line,

they do not harvest me in star clusters.
    I am a woman expecting a baby.

At the moshav,
covered with moss,
I rested with the farmers.

One said teacher shortages
will render the curriculum invalid.

Another thought the photograph
was a prod to destroy
paraffin oil.

Yet another knew the setback
was termite-eating
in the way of the heads of comets.

I smoked the wedge
of cold air suddenly blowing in
from the octopus-intervals.

This is the official beginning of the—
both ovaries? the White House? having an egg-shaped illusion?

They came over and tried to cheer me up.
The movie, in its final version, had its arms outstretched.

What is this artistic establishment you speak of?
The plays smuggled out of China are assassin thrillers,

but that doesn't make them suitable as gray-white cumulus clouds,
that doesn't make them substitutes for cooking and heating food.

My friends were a telephone connection breaking up
the semiarid discussion about the little joke (Pascal's Wager)

which at the time some of us took very seriously indeed.
The passing of the years became a little eccentric, like trench warfare.

I crossed the street.
At this period of time,

the passing seconds were
like penicillin, little

magicians who had fled
imprisonment.

I mended quill pens.
The blue mold (very poor),

equal to one hundredth
of a paintbrush,

put me to mint-sleep.
The flying saucers

were professionally engaged
by clerks (and authors)

of the time as hardness,
hard alloy rods,

as pendulums
of the clews of sails,

ringing in our ears
as graphite forecasts.

(Penmanship) the antennae of my proud grandma,
    the underparts of her large etiquette in the legal idiom:

I was proud of her, her incisors and Mongolian neck.

Thirteen quatrains at a fountain.
The 1970s were a Romanic language,
a nose with a high bridge, a civil law
in many countries even today.

We who
captured Tobruk stuffed ourselves
with jam.

Rome (winter-sports center)
was not built in a day, nor in a verbal
attack of pelvic structures (resembling
lizards).

Alcohol (day of Saturn) occupies
the gastronome's every second week,
transmitting memories of the writer first,
the scientist second, lubricating skin and
hair and timber.

Across a marked shovel
on a table, the wing is attached, the lost wing
that shouts, "blueberries need acid soil."

I speak of solar energy
  as a stenographer.

Puddings, pastry, mincemeat,
  the rise of the suede alteration,

vaguely to recognize me as such-and-such
  a character in a linking of

sentences. My head is jammed
  up against the back of the sofa.

I view your leather-tablature
  when you are naked and tabby,

in the atmosphere of the punctual
  dining room, when you are

resting from studies. Your penis
  occurs in the frame of fourteen

working days, each of which is
  uncouth, like political constitutions.

I unclasp your fingers from my hair.
  The middle ear, weepingly, is black video.

Our parents knew about insulin
(which was beside the point) when they
sprinkled us with flakes of pastry.

You slipped me pale green gemstones,
your refuge from wallflower-mountains,
and I besieged your chemical alphabet.

The ball I hit carried well in the park.
The lady at the tea table showed interest in us.
Our mathematics were motorcycle-imitative.

When I told my father about the street gang
(sitting as a committee), he said any two men have
little in common, even if their tight curls

suggest a crisis has developed. Read me
the rhubarb-crisp play, whose knife is a knife of
cloths, and color-blindedness, a woman

resembling a dam. Children learn best by doing
(Chinese calligraphy), the sinister film of dew
in the morning describes the shape of our skulls.

I heard (a severe form of malaria) when woolen knitwear
    (songbird to two kings of Iraq) a fix-it shop's melody

(anise and peppercorn), my flaccid hand in your flaccid hand,
and 300 sparklers and epithets locked in the foundry. This

    is what I heard: a cascade like a fountain of glengarry-breath,
the harvest of the 1890s when a person's eyes were *glas* and gondolas

gliding past slippery gray. Glasnost was far off, so goodhearted
Russian propaganda (the music of intimate PCB levels, relaxed

    gangsters, and fishing in the consonant-harbor) swept over
us without changing our mood of iconolatry, our scribbling on the back

    of the stove. What is thought of as curing jaundice? Perhaps
the main parts of the (climbing-ivied) tusks, the heat and the dust.

The stamps I loaded into
  a taxi, cutting light into logs

(the crowds of controversial sidewalk-businessmen):
  a grump and a dump of holiday sadness,

the mastodon that was Malawi's icon
  slicing into the mewing of (Monday) gulls.

A sport where you gentlemen-confectioners—
  chiefly for knives and sword blades? no—
for the joy of the stream, for the upholstery,
          produce in sums of money amateurs
(predatory water beetles) who share the long long dance.

These are the parts of the language. Death, in my will,
          is a chamber without a chair, a fine without heat,
all of us concerned for the smaller evidence (exhaust fumes
          of personal sentiment), the umpire's finger

going up like the stock exchange produced in cans.
  The ball resting against the cushion of fuchsia flowers
draping my legs, the size of botanist-mafias (Bob Dylan,
all of the greats), those very sounds, great auks, parish

churches to the tuft-grass apes. The village green (whose
tales are full of humor) deters attack on the major poets in
          their 16th-century moods, as we equal diminutive-
invasions, the leap in the park, the leap for the lock of hair.

I went to Miami Beach,
molasses shaped to the cornice
of tongue-climate. There,
the ant lions and snake flies
came in from offshore pedicures,

the holiday was a vital area
of psychoanalysis. Dry leaves are
aging. The schlubs (identified
as Homer's Troy) are members of
the secret police, skeleton-water.

I am afraid of:
  spraddle, the tartufo-spree

of the Tarim, evaporating,
with not much of a defined bed,

evaporating into pollen sacs,
cartoons. I am afraid of:

thatches of trout lilies,
  making me stay away from school.

What is not covered by insurance?
The weeklong wiggle of the hips.

I am afraid of gliders,
  I refuse to drop closer to the ground.

After the fall of Jerusalem—
after laissez-passer at the Wailing Wall—

the black river out of gear,
the one who worships idle threats.

When my mother—
through the arrows of idle-memory—
became hybrid

back-formation,
            of lower rank than the angels,

then I brought bad lack (wryneck)
to translating her ear,

and in the local tango (or polka),
the infection, they said,

was minuscule:

                              like the dry
monsoon, a simpler sugar.

On the order of Janis Joplin: these
feast days (the appalling loss of life I knew
in the third battle) are theater-colonies,

where I cannot take action to prevent accidents,
I cannot, in the evenings, startle with Pop Art,
I cannot be a small sharp blade to stiff leather.

This advanced stage of
1960s jet planes (venomous-spines)
is less exact sadism, marine
wool, you get the rough edge?

The falconer, pepper-needy man,
by jazz or pavement as a bomb,

a gargoyle having small breasts,
stones in which the fruit is ripe.

I learned handwriting as a single member
of a class of pilots.

For the storage of oil
(the death of the insured person) the observed
values are mouth-central.

Explain to me
this language spoken by six million people.

I am a full month of the moon (my never-never
land at the south celestial pole), and my fleshy
cheek pads

are soon to see the bladed African tool.

Blazing homes! An alteration
of postage with palm turned outward
and a steel bill.

These odes celebrate XYZ affairs.
The bagpipes give you new finishes,
they make of you a rose-pink delta.

A little liquid, a steam of gas,
the throbbing of a tortoise judge,
my name made of silk ribbons, silk hair.

Decorate me with irregular drops.
Gut, lungs, yolk sac.
I am still breathing all-black paintings.

The red seas (yielding this timber) are inferior
to teapoy patterns, the poets noted
for their descriptions of childhood.

In various states of undress, I am undone!
The last thing is to pay a respectful visit
to the railway grit of the human brain.

Bald argyle, a fine spray, fission of
the critical mass where your lightning
forbids masculine tone,

                                        the mists
of Zeus being made to support athletes,
anthems, books formed of coral.

The dragon artist drafted legal documents.
My mother, who thought of Allah reluctantly,
like a drag race lacking heavy loads,

is a character
from *A Study in Scarlet*, or *The Hound of the Baskervilles*,
because of her feet of euphony which are to
perfumery what Nazi disfavor is.

To live to the icy
surface of 100-plus, preserved in Juba (euphoria),
one must be a bird of many feathered hats, one must owe
fealty to the collages of found photos hiding under

umbrellas of chronic pain.

To learn to die like a goldfish
(happy and peaceful when the hair hails a cab) is to
designate a star at the lower slopes, where the landscape
has no buttons missing,

and the soil has white breast patches.

All the little people of the monarch's dance—
we are being invaded by champagne running out—

the invaders are a detachment of villagers whose
Urdu is not quite what you would hope it would be,

but their fetal abnormalities (and other containers) we
hope we can forgive. I tried to enliven my mother

with the help of Voltaire-paper wrappers, the immensity
of wool and mohair, hiding from the Endlösung

that never comes. Winter, winter of stony fish,
winter of debris flickering across the yellow-shafted

face, tell me something about warm waters, tell me
if the house will grow on me when the invaders

become invisible with the sun. What number of copies
of the book is just right? The witness is vague and arch.

The litany of 100 liquid songs,
each one of which is the price of a candela,

placed on rooftops (to hum a lullaby/
soothing drink) on the morning of the destroyed

horse-divided-lobes (the matchbook imam
who ran away to Canada), and each of

the songs an eye in the sun, a mute swan
(never on Friday) listening to the firearm.

Perspectivism:
a person's body entering hygiene,
the degree of slope at which I break,

separated by the distance of (one step) players
playing the same ball.
The exterior noise

native to my gait (heraldic tincture) is a noise
of silver-haired card games, in which we waste
our Fridays arranging the fourfold pearls.

I cannot—
this garment, a griffin and a filly—

affixing stamps to the album,
I saw outside the window the beginning of a word—

A child's teeth, pearly white,
forming the names of magnesium and probity—

I cannot feed on prey—
the undirected movements of my cells.

The language of my monkeys is the realm of a queen.
She retired in 1983, kinematics of a German children's

garden, the head of the river of the water-babies dense
with imprisoned gods. The hindmost person does not drag

(ladies who lunch, in Karachi's posh ladder tournaments)
anything of the parts of the living images of the food-

dispensing saints. The roofs require limited manpower,
not so true of the mannikin-godowns, male servants with a

safety rope tied around their necks. Their stories range
from lurid colors to lunar mantles, they want us to believe

that ash-melancholy expression comes to them unpracticed,
that they are the mongers we see from the top of the minaret.

I admit I will call you Monday.

The aromatic foliage contracts (poor thing),
as soon as I make my promise,

the days we call nones are all we have in common,
like plates of stones for the noon office.

The afternoon adhan comes (off-screen lover) when I
am wandering the oceans:

                                        dear Sonia Delaunay (glassmaker),
the pagan gods are always three syllables short, one of which
is shale, one is paradox, and the last the sedative lens.

this is paradise (his book. a book). a blow
from the rabbit-fist. generations of Romanians
(rooks) have stated. being sated. reborn
as Parvati, in purple-flowered S. purpurea.
the smells of the aluminum-alloy satin-soaked
south. the american south. customers in a particular.
listening to the live broadcast, the curved.
balconies do not meet, do not meet. a gun holster,
molten lead. what if I should trust? you people.
a taunt. a racist gesture. slogging. home to paradise.
too much moving from one needle. living flesh. sloka.

Concerning the bloody quarrel between the sons (should
we see a doctor who can stretch the elastic?)

they won't streetlight
me if they think what I have to say follows the theme at
shorter and shorter intervals

(the rubber will stretch).

My
bones are loosely joined, my Star of David increases in energy,
just when you think my voice resembles a human voice.

The darkness
of this moving-skeleton country

may take the form of an alphabet,
a one-day bicycle race,

perhaps small crystals in fruit storage,
or the suspicion on your forehead.

When the sun finally oscillates,
the dog croaks to crinkled foliage.

Skin markings are falling off,
the mainsprings of the disaster movie.

Methodically, the desert shrinks figures.
Staccato, the note, the rest, the note, the rest…

Adam signed on the dotted…
(she is a cousin of the mazzard and the morello)

the owner of steel magnolias
you sweeten the fingerboard by your bowing,
your plucking, your long rounded body
and Appalachian dulcimer:

reverence to the saints and angels,
the dull lamplight du jour.

Much time has elapsed.

The lining of the artery is definitive.

The risk of extinction (are you deliberately
trying to estrange readers?) of the
lens aperture, featherweight
cuspings in tracery…

                              The work of art
is a promise of something…partly wooded,
partly a person other than the other.

The flower is forgotten by the wearer.

I sat on the long bench without a back.
In some compost (I'm from Hartford) some
phylactery for large antelopes...
                                                  gemmae,
let there be peace, light from the shadow, from
the piece of gospel music, the north side of
the altar, at which the blond gossamer—
                                                            was I
thinking of your hair, your Cappadocia-apartheid
hair singing of the pseudonyms of Alexei
Maksimovich...
      the first syllable, mistaken for god, God.

In which the alphabet is
a card box. The heart or upper
opening of my stomach. The
carcass of newspapers littering my
conspicuous crest, east and west,
the shape of phenol decay.

Andalusia's rhombic prisms,
 the dwelling place in the afternoon,
 what was your name again?

Agape among old friends
 (I too was called for aliyah),
 who do not steam the letters.

Others will rally around.
 Some moths (jurors empaneled)
 circle the hills around the city.

Eat your final blanquette.

A dance like a gavotte, born in
India or South Africa, my faint bouquet
of almonds.

    I know the harmonium
from the outburst of the territorial
forest.

    A promenade of one,
upon bouncy artificial grass.

Kafur, in bathrooms, sprayed over
cooking grills, my pinkish doorstep,
the larva of carrageen.

To be replaced by a knowledge bone
during the community's grammatical base,
and then in the monastery…

pore-cloggers, close relatives from
the hotel, who put me under discussion
as winter solstice approaches.

                                        I hear their
every word mistaking "illegal" for confraternité,
I am still picking up the phone,

the critter that has lived in this shack,
the foreign student searching for the brothel.

To my dismay, she did not leave me.

Take me to Crete in February,
where we are bound to get fireworks.

Who among us is not a serf or a slave?

The fumes lit the cat free, the hexachords
of chronic pain are illuminated by blind luck,
I have gambled with the goldfish bowl.

The distance, from gryphons of stone
stuck in place, from the young Muslim woman
who grows up in such few square meters
(the star Delta Gruis is fruit topped with cookie dough),
is my punishment.

Bright star, accidental digger,
tell me about the margins of the fronds, other windows,
other screens, other suns: I'd like a stroke or a seizure,
I'd like a six-petaled volcano to be my travel document.

The news, from *Izvestia*, is bad.
To grow up like Primo Levi you must first
be a leviathan of the deep. Dovetail
mortise, being fixed in, there is no village
left that hasn't yet read *Elmer Gantry*.

The wolf, the wolf, siege engine to contraceptives,
the company's workers are abstract units,
lexemes, mere polished stones who compile
dictionaries (such as the capital of Tibet),
for shelter from the long-coated wolf.

The elements of a piece of writing
derived from light and law and ritual

are no different than the interest payable
to escape wheels, emblazoned tracksuits

that make of logography a bullet forever
lodged near the chromosome-pea-spine.

My earliest memory is of the madrasa (naked eye)
    where I learned the overall structure of languages after dark

and malefic Saturn having its eye on me, the pistil of Brunei,
    and the ways of the malkaya drinking fruity wine and swallowing blood.

The nylon bristles shrivel.
Theirs is hair exposed to sunlight.
The whorls of my wind-pollinated milk
satisfy my earthly cochlea. I hear
the wind of the morning gift, I cut
to the white juicy flesh of the musket,
the moment the ball is played.

The Art of Love

I

I moderate tight shell jackets as leptotenes,
spit and polish the rude dining room, fix

the candelabrum above your forked head,
model Le Corbusier's metalline materials.

2

And what have you done for me, rove beetle?
Scant is the civility you show to my Bengal

lights, though I give you the benefit of the doubt
even in long johns, even at my Nabokov nadir.

3

OGPU, which replaced the Cheka, which was
in turn replaced by the NKVD: I am no ogre

though I keep the running totals in my head
as security ruse, the mythos of progression.

4

What are the tangibles in our new situation?
Last night you rose above the flotilla, in your

crib made from spacesuits, and I canceled
all my dates with canary wine in the newsroom.

5

Define surrealism for me. Decorous clothing
suitable to clouds? St. Thomas à Becket as

archeological site? Knout flogging me until I
go past Nevada as rhinestone? Newlyweds?

6

I could be Sherlock if you lie to me. Or I could
be Tartuffe, or Tarzan, or Tartarus, because I am

vin ordinaire, you think, o Viola!, a man of forty
foundering like sheep, ohm or om or Omaha drab.

7

And you would be right. Trudge on, El Paso
night, make those sounds of hard granules, fly

the flag high, sink into the long legs and neck
of the flamingo while I flail in the paddies.

8

Elkhart is an industrial city in northern Indiana,
noted also for the manufacture of musical instru-

ments. The police dog was all too polite to me,
first native-born composer, young pink feather.

9

You are my redeemer at noon, we conjoin to in-
filtrate the inexplicable melee, my cheers melt

into gasps of admiration, we read at the festival
of Purim, feeding the quintuple muse of tragedy.

10

A singer with the properties of a magnetic cir-
cuit, the high relief of raising money for famine:

in the Bible I was son of Noah, I had the modern
sense of the right to vote, toughened by erections.

II

If you could see me as the winding sheet that has
been going round and round the expectation of a

Prussian advance, if you could see me as expelled
from the chest, a go-slow passage from a novel.

12

Then we would not be viewed as bumpkins, we
would be buoyant color wheels, coltsfoot that

treated the consequences of bouldering, and every
hour we would bow before the basket-of-gold.

13

Yesterday I quite exceeded the load factor, don't
you think? Obstreperous patterns of rafting make

me want to raffle myself off for a scholarship
to the fine arts, or to attend to the cold rain tree.

14

Do you want to change the spelling of the second
word associated with my name? It is all the same

to me, I have lately not manned the sternpost, I
couldn't even tell you who did the third reading.

15

When we were not looking, or thinking out loud,
when we were the thirty-nine articles all this

week, when we were wing oysters not asleep,
the birds of Ludwigshafen at last got their lumps.

16

Satanic ritual abuse, William Saroyan's mem-
oirs, the woman bearing me a pygmy, Morgan

le Fay in the caste system, the 11:00 pm last call:
will you now treat me as the stranger I can be?

17

Quite conceivably, we have erred in being so
clinical about botulin, and also lawn bowling

according to the law, and the pinhole camera
seeing only pink: let us exit the school bus.

18

Silent we will flee, unseen by the trucemakers,
buttinskies who light international candles and

are blind to the cankerworm. I am still the blue-
eyed boy, you are aurora borealis or could be.

19

What is the one fantasy you never realized?
My family tree includes hobbits and Ho Chi

Minh alike, leading to me, the jaywalker, Jazz
Age knockout hiding lag screws in my mouth.

20

I didn't catch you when you struck the false
note because I didn't want to, not because of

acute nostalgia, and not because the old empty
words, like "to," stand forever at concert pitch.

21

Yes, the moon's blueberry computer animation,
Blum and Blume and Bloom all blurbing my

new book (what blue pencil?), yes, anchorage
among Adélie penguins, what more can I do?

22

It’s the problem of insomnia I do not share
with you, but only with Elamites whose eight-

fold path is visible like groupware, it’s the
inhaler that saturates my clinical left brain.

23

When at last we depart it will be legendary.
As all deaths are legendary, all loves are leg-

endary, in the mind of the planisphere, in
the fellowship denoting a little of the skeleton.

24

Observe the sitzmark I left when I plundered
the logic of temperance. You tempt me, again,

toward menorrhagia, toward crepuscular act-
ing, even as I lose the flask in the dust storm.

25

What in God's name are you doing up there?
Ortega y Gasset's works include *The Revolt of*

The Masses, wherein he proposed leadership by
an intellectual elite. I run a slouching orphanage.

26

Napoleon took over the island, Toussaint died in prison
in France, a titanic tower of garbage emerged above

the weather in low spirits, I fell by the wayside as your
terminology became more complicated and worn.

27

I climbed Mount Fujiyama as something less than a
fuel rod, before my days of chemical abuse and photo-

graphic memory. It is stressful sometimes to take the
straw polls concerning the uterus and its wind chimes.

28

The Jacobins were ruthless? How about the great
Jain teachers or holy men, posing in gran turismos

like nabobs of counterpoint, chastising me for the
tests of stamina I put them through as deckhands.

29

Surely love in its Canetti strands decomposes like
a mercer's which is not renewable, not scandalized,

not even squirting perfume. Surely we have the pres-
ence of mind for a textbook emergency descent.

30

You do not fit into any of the typologies I know.
Viewed as an exhibition of la vie de Bohème you

leave much to be desired, your phantom vigil lights
flicker on and off, picked up by the frigate on the sea.

31

Do dabbling ducks compose purple passages? No,
I didn't think so, and copperheads don't have to be

poisonous, ingots are not always oblong, the lead
time can be the end time, the median full of meat.

32

So we come to yet another crossroads, where the
rare earth elements become manifest, swallows grow

over the house like infidelity, or ink, and the celesta
strikes and turns into a dogtooth violet, or blister rust.

33

Domestication is practicum among unreal dons of
febrifuge, every farm I have known, or hot spring,

wants to reduce me to house brand, doesn't let me
rappel down the newel post as aristocrat dying alone.

34

Please stop at the flue stop. I am pinned to the ferry
wheel though I tried to seduce only *Izvestia*, or at

times the merchandize of Nostradamus, but writers
will have peace talks with snow cones and vinyl too.

35

I am not known for documentaries on marine life.
That's true. When the cows come home the living

stone metabolizes into a piece of eight, your wages
and mine are paid off by restaurateurs at the top tier.

Sometime after midnight I want to learn to write beautiful prose poems.

The sun comes out, we know, logically, that it is not the sun that is arriving,
but such errors are frequent.

A student of Dante invokes his vision of hell
in *The Divine Comedy* and is struck with blindness.

An oracle foretells
that she would have a son who would kill her father.

Danzig, the German
name for Gdansk, which do you prefer?

I travel to one of the Galilean
moons of Jupiter, date a police officer, one on each side of the crankshaft.

The beauty of the stone flatters the young investigator's eyes in the flatlands.

A Muslim nobleman or person of high status, a native governor during the time of the Mughal empire, contemplating his navel.

The breathtaking beauty of nature.

The rhythm of a line of verse.

A rudimentary leaf, feather, or bract.

He walks confidently behind them and trucks on through: have you gone troppo?

I'm a dyed-in-the-wool patriot, the film's opening is an echt pop snob event, her hands claw my shoulders.

Can we reach a point in the business venture where the profits equal the losses?

I hate doing this, but I need the bread, I am the oldest known fossil bird, I have mastered two knots, the clove hitch, and the sheet bend.

Ice cubes clink in crystal glasses, my alleged quest to make it with the world's most attractive woman.

I am trying to decide if I should major in drama or English, each of a number of small plots of vegetation.

Her husband remains at the beach condo raising money for famine relief.

Tilde, as in señor, or São Paulo, or white noise, perhaps one whose faulty grandeur among the creosote bushes grows like violinmakers in Cremona observing cynical everglades.

The outer layer of the cerebrum, the outer layer of the cosmological argument, which I won, and you won, and then the cosmopolitans took over as overshadowing press releases.

Uncritical adherence to present-day attitudes, especially the tendency to interpret past events in terms of modern values and concepts.

You are squeaky-
clean, soul brother, kiss the trousseau with the excitement of seeing a live leopard.

The counter tells you how many pictures you have taken, and also tells you the small harbor bustled with boats.

Someone's number is up.

Someone is into necrophilia.

A

referee is referenced, citing literature up to 1900.

War can only be explained as spun
silk unconscious of its aims, the uncertainty principle inherent in viscera, a cocktail made of vodka, coffee liqueur, and milk served on ice.

Wear the white belt when in doubt.

A spy who achieves over a long period an important position within the security defenses of a country.

A fungal growth that causes decay, due to age or damp conditions.

A small burrowing insectivorous mammal with dark velvety fur, a long muzzle, and very small eyes.

Soft loose earth?

I bite back a tart reply.

The tar pit of municipal poverty.

Two men are targeted by the attackers from the initial letters of Tom Swift's electric rifle.

The committee does not expect members to be put to any expense.

There are over 900 living species of bats, the whole evening is a carnival of fun, a wave that forms over a submerged offshore reef or rock, the Indian movie industry based in Bombay.

I serve you tetrazzini in Spanish Town, water slaps against the boat, farmers view the rise in rabbit numbers with concern.

She follows, slipping on the wet rock.

They wend their way across the city.

You are still seeing the profession through rose-colored glasses, the fresh air will soon pass.

Four months of violent confrontation between government and opposition forces. Confucian egg white, the ballet fails to congeal as a single oeuvre, compared with false coral snake.

It was the capital of the Inca empire until the Spanish conquest in 1533, until the continuous welded rail, until a cyanide group bonded to the central cobalt atom of a cobalamin molecule.

Speckled brown plumage, a conspicuous crimson throat-band, and a rufous belly.

I am a cutoff valve, a concealed informant, the defense played deep.

Stephen loses the first three holes to Eric at Jackson Hole. I can't get down, she hollers.

If you can't get hold of some ripe tomatoes, add some tomato puree. I reach up to the nearest branch that seems likely to hold my weight.

The ship is holding a southeasterly course.

He explores the interpenetration of solids and voids in his series of "transparent" sculptures of the 1920s, has a flowing shaggy mane and takes little part in hunting, which is done cooperatively by the females.

A block of risen linoleum.

The optimistic mood of the sixties, a thing that is or may be chosen, an orange glow in the sky, error, pallor, terror.

Naval glory strikes me as paltry.

The consensus

is that the palm should go to Doerner.

Young pigeon, resembling a dove, the palpable bump at the bridge of the nose.

Named from the anthology le parnasse contemporain (1866), he commits a burglary while on parole, scraping food from coral and other hard surfaces.

I am a percipient interpreter of the public mood.

If

I do not perceive myself as disabled, nobody should, stickers bearing peppy slogans.

Eve perches on the side of the armchair, he is generally accepted as the author of the satyricon.

A woman with silvery blond hair, Sylvia Plath, the best play is to lead the three of clubs, she also acted in movies such as she-devil, all is not roses in the firm today.

The unseasonal sighting of a cuckoo.

Earth of Siena.

Infinite progression in a finite space, English Creole, Temne, and other West African languages, sign someone on.

Typically living in running water, the district attorney denotes electrons and orbitals in genealogies of daughters, in travel timetables, penny or pence of predecimal currency: the fourth file from the left, as viewed from White's side of the board.

Longfin dace.

A crane fly, perhaps imitative of a small child's first syllables, a craftsman said to be the inventor of carpentry.

Her hand hovers over the console.

How do they play?

How is your vacation?

How are the children?

I'm not sure how fast to go.

Accused of infidelity, she confesses and is beheaded.

Perhaps from Sioux háo or Omaha hou.

He is chiefly remembered for his poems culled in a shropshire lad, she refuses to give houseroom to the canvas her brother has brought.

A seat for riding on the back of an elephant or camel, an inhabitant of the extreme north, analogous to a cube in three dimensions.

A tree frog of a widespread genus.

A most unusual passage like a hymn to the great outdoors, exaggerated, hyperbolical, placing so much emphasis on willpower.

Icky boys with all their macho strutting.

Being a scientist is enjoyable, and winning a Nobel is icing on the cake.

The part of the mind in which innate instinctive impulses and primary processes are manifest, compared with ego and superego, a pancake made with grated potato, a communal one in a camp or barracks, no letter appears twice in the same row or column.

Belonging to the final stages of a person's life, the project has had low cash flows in latter years, the book is built around the story of flood and treason and cooking and percussive instruments and a cross.

Larry works himself into a lather and shouts at the mayor: they are treated as menials, on a level with cooks!

An early form of capacitor consisting of a glass jar with layers of metal foil on the outside and inside, containing details of law and ritual, the lion, the witch, and the wardrobe.

A linear narrative in one's pockets.

Hundreds of telegrams line the walls.

We follow the history of a family through the male line, through the end of an axle.

A parchment inscribed with religious texts and attached in a case to the doorpost of a Jewish house as a sign of faith: an American in Paris.

A throng of cats and kittens mewing to be fed, the use or study of poetic meters, a wine bottle of eight times the standard size, complete identification with the part.

He performs a brief mime of someone fencing.

Do you mimic me like a current of water in a millrace?

Am I likely to be deterred by finger-wagging?

I write a letter in my mind.

People mill about the room, shaking hands, talking about his expansionist policies, the god of light, best-known for works on American culture.

Newer pilots often leave their mixture rich during an entire flight, such questions are not asked in mixed company, especially not when the patient moans and opens his eyes.

Oh God, a dazzling montage of the movie's central banquet scene, specific to one antigen!

A person or business that has a monopoly.

A railroad in which the track consists of a single rail, and only one buyer.

We decide to go to the movies.

The novel shows minimal concern for narrative movement, self-sufficient in terms of key, tempo, and structure, marking the country's move to independence, a field of grass grown for hay.

Making myself an Arab, the mouth of the bottle, a fine semi-opaque fabric similar to muslin, I'll never open up about you.

Burning herb.

Despite the high prices, goods are moving.

Machines can do everything that we can do, held between the knees and played with a bow like a cello, we share similar musical tastes.

A problem inherent in any attempt to read science fiction.

Narcissus, I love you like the genus daffodil, you are an important center of Japanese buddhism, your company has narrowed down the candidates for the job to two, you are swami and friends, you are the man-eater of malgudi, you are the painter of signs, you breathe abdication through your nostrils, you are a state of stupor and a bomb containing napalm and a baby's diaper and a stolen apple blossom.

I hate doing this, but I need the bread: the Caribbean sea breaking gently on the shore.

His health breaks down under the strain of overwork.

The blistering heat of the desert.

A blinding fastball.

A bibliography of my publications.

Via French from dialect Arabic abu shīr.

Guests will bid for pieces of fine jewelry, an excessive adherence to the literal interpretation of the Bible.

There is no lack of entertainment aboard ship, there is a lack of parking space in town.

A lizard of a large family to which most European lizards belong, the labor-intensive task of tagging each item in the store, one of the recurrent pains felt by a woman during childbirth, milky in appearance.

The institute houses an outstanding library of 35,000 volumes on the fine arts, not visible from the earth, but sometimes coming into view, the drug already licensed for human use.

It is the forerunner of the pound, it is freed from enemy occupation, it is the liquid song of the birds, very common.

Consult the list of drugs on page 326 to spark the magic recovery.

There is no need to martyr myself again.

My fifteen books of epigrams, in a variety of meters, reflect the high tide, Apollo in the contest for flute playing, the cadency of the fourth son, the founding of modern communism: horse feathers, duck soup, and a night at the opera.

Dandelion greens, mustard greens, and radicchio.

A high plateau in southern Colorado, with the remains of many prehistoric Pueblo Indian dwellings: a circle passing through the celestial poles and the zenith of a given place on the earth's surface.

There's method in that man's meshugaas.

The high-lying parlando of Siegfried's narration, visitors can partake of golfing or clay pigeon shooting.

Be sparing.

He commits a burglary while on parole.

The peanut gallery's probing of my privacy, widely roasted and salted and eaten as a snack, a greenish blue color like that of a peacock's neck: don't peck at your food, eat a whole mouthful.

Don't repair to the tranquility of the nearby café, don't appear solid and three-dimensional.

I reappear as a person who repairs vehicles, machinery, or appliances, I don't know why caffeine's suddenly got such a bad rep, I don't intend to let history repeat itself.

A lathe that rounds chair legs.

The latest attacks have been roundly condemned by campaigners for peace.

A florid passage of runs in classical music for a solo virtuoso, the players betting on the number at which the ball comes to rest, she tries to tell me she feels rotten, a run-through of the whole show.

The property has been allowed to run down, his conversation is seasoned liberally with exclamation points and punch lines.

I seclude myself up here for a life of study and meditation.

The secondary or Mesozoic era.

Literally ear of wheat, in the hand of the goddess.

The magician may cast a spell on himself.

I propound a riddle about the three ages of man, aromatic leaves, bark, and fruit: this organization does sterling work for youngsters.

I find the fraternity's teachings sterile, a sound that is directed through two or more speakers.

Old men swig from bottles of plum brandy.

I'd rather carry on in my own sweet
way, an interval spanning three consecutive notes in a diatonic scale, the Uto-Aztecean
language of the people, the electric kool-aid acid test, the bonfire of the vanities, and
a man in full.

He got away—bully for him!

With the onset of puberty, I become
new as opposed to paper currency, these acts exclude the deer and commonable
cattle.

My wife deals with my private correspondence.

Don't have a cow—it's no
big deal!

These companies have deep pockets and don't mind spending to get their
projects off the ground, the question in dispute is altogether insignificant.

My re-
search has moved into the realm of fantasy.

The moon maiden is one of a number of
lunar inhabitants, with whom I get along famously, like a pot of gold, like the dia-
lect of Akan.

Many valuable drugs have been recognized first as poisons.

Language
is a bomb designed to cause a fire, a fire at a hotel, a fire in the heart of the warbler.

Gut flora.

The Gutenberg Bible.

Gutta-percha or Gustavus Adolphus laying the foundations of the state.

I can always appear nude, I'm never too inhibited.

Your vocal cords, which is to say legal capacity, are the weaker side of the body.

My road's the first left.

The story of a saint's life.

I do at least six loads of washing a week, in textual references, lines, lunar modules, resembling liver in color and consistency.

The Horatian ode has an intricate governing meter, and so do the six million people in Sumatra and elsewhere, and so does the venomous American pit viper.

The wind must have dehydrated and mummified my body.

I am several processors at different stages of execution.

Sweden and its fellow neutrals.

Nine-fold increase in the amount of traffic.

Shall we keep an open line to the White House, shall we act our way out of the paper bag?

All our gods collectively, paper wasps in the end, tests to detect cancer of the cervix or uterus, or extinct leaks.

36

You look in the mirror, dismayed at the hunting that has led to excess butterfly pupa and the mis-

timing of checkered tablecloths. I take shelter in a mazelike building with no windows and doors.

37

Do you mean my present period of service? The
sniper fired and hit a rookie whose fragrant life-

span was only seconds longer than mine, in the
rewriting of history, in his methods of payment.

38

I designed these step pyramids you see in the de-
sert of Amy Lowell and James Joyce, the film's

religious imagery is like a child learning to speak
by imitation: I am organized like the Freemasons.

39

Many spirits of ranks lower than the angels dance
a jig, break the tenth of a yuan. I can be a serious

pest of timber, my bracelets jingle when your hear-
ing contains the language of the people of infinity.

40

Make me lighter, brighter, make me a drop in the
uterus in the last days of cigarettes, a glass of

light Hungarian wine. I attract a lot of criticism
just as in some lights your shirt looks beautiful.

41

I can be unchaste, promiscuous, the velocity
of light in a vacuum, prisoner outside my cell.

Engineers are working to locate the fault, so
help them catch lobsters, park on the rooftop.

42

I wrote back then in a declamatory avant-garde style, passing in one direction at maximal speed.

Your green sports car, shining with sequins and metallics, is in the mood of lawful pentathlons.

43

But we are not the same motherwort when it
comes down to it, I have been attracted to show-

biz like a millipede with elongated body, I will
not nag anyone to do the housework in style.

44

Once upon a time, in streamlined housing, a nativity play, nods to pantomime, chemical actions

symbolizing the innate goodness of humanity, a music of noble arches and contracted adverbs.

45

I do often forget the past like I ignore the note of
scorn in your branch of psychiatry, though I don't

yet design my own clothes, I don't have a passion
for gardens, and I don't have perforated initials.

46

Perhaps the wall of a ripened ovary? I burst
through the pleasant smell and secondary stress,

the odd placement of a hydrogen atom before a
carbon atom, I burst through satsuma phobias.

47

This primal scene was enacted for the rent-a-
crowd, the representatives of trucks beyond

repair, the lime-rich protein-saturated voice.
I ran the tape back and ended with satinwood.

48

I'm just spitballing a few ideas. When the spirits
of the dead visit me in floral silks, I admire their

subculture of white lilies and official titles, but my
conscience does not suffer me to expect more.

49

We can create our own subordinate country of small
panels, pedals for two riders, estrogen antagonists,

tiny scalelike leaves borne on slender branches of
thermal efficiency, knitted for warmth and comfort.

50

Of course I am a thief, like a traffic island caught
in a vignette of weighted averages (theft is a propo-

sition as incomplete as a wedding cake), of course I
am hamstrung by lack of knowledge of hind wings.

51

Give me your hand. On it I will write with a pen,
the one the puppet gave me to listen to, like a tele-

phone attached to blame. I read your predecessor's
reports, they reeked of the labor camp's big heart.

52

Somebody wrote a novel and ninety years later I
read it in the full bloom of youth. A landsman is a

person unfamiliar with the sea or sailing, children
learn language like the salty breeze at Land's End.

53

Why do I call it the art of love? Why not the meson
that passes through my calm attitude and makes of

my many moons unprecedented degrees of precision
for dating rocks, rocks like my rasplike many teeth.

54

No, that definition didn't work. I call love the local
rag when it lacks finish, ancient Roman law leading

to the domes of American Motors, sansevieria we ad-
mire in the stellar wind for the stencil around the door.

55

Sales are up, which is a step in the right direction.
Sales of poetry, I mean, cowboys and Indians in a

brazen illegal business breaking away from the ar-
bor made of consonants whose faith is Abraham.

56

Mathematicians are homeless before they know it,
inventors become recurrent symbols of the alumni

formerly known as Geiger counters or geisha girls,
nighthawk poets dot i's and cross t's in hysteresis.

57

Like ignis fatuus our love rose from the steamy marsh-
es like the nautch of OCD, which you have to admit

is better than octopuses strangling our pulverulent re-
lief map, the stage fright of this our second childhood.

58

Today is Thanksgiving and it is the first time I am
out of words. I once tried Tibetan Buddhism like a

disorder of the ticker tape, I would hear the tick-tock
of vowel points back when the dervishes debouched.

59

Define Debussy's quality of sadness. It is float
glass reflecting Greta Garbo's reclusive retirement,

it is the Jesse window opening on to lorikeets bask-
ing in a melba sun for the melodrama of it.

60

None of my definitions work, of course, as long as
the mons veneris is an ordinal number we do battle

with, and the physiognomy of our known and un-
known precipices comes back as the roving dream.

61

My second home is moral science. Yours? When
you make wood seasoned to snuff out the voltage

of snoozing, when the totalitarian tropics dress
up in moody organdy: what an oriflamme orbit!

62

The masculine is the norm for me, or used to be,
at the limit point. The lineage of jailbreakers tore

apart the infula hiding my inner grammarian, but
I kept my feet in both camps, fooling with cameras.

63

It would be fine to spend a night as a black-backed
jackal, whose spirit of overstrung pit-a-pat would

be just like my heart dismissing the scandals of old-
er patients, scaling up the laboratory procedures.

64

Screaming electron microscope. Dry and flaky
revealing skimpy clothing, Tarkovsky's unconstitu-

tional housekeeping, the hounds of Gray code, all
the ways we take at face value the lying handcuffs.

65

Did you see the neutron star? It exploded inside
the open market when the satiety centers dropped

into their magisterial styles of questioning. Did you
see how the goldfinch set up its little ergosphere?

66

I am erratic like the island upon which the logicians
macerate oral histories, repackaged as renunciation,

which doesn't interest me in the least. A frogman can
know something of style, etched in our hoatzin mind.

67

This is an actual place or natural setting in which
my broadcast is being made, I am a key mover in

making this successful conference happen. Moxie
is just another word for a psalm to Prussian blue.

68

Proxemics, whose study is provisory, like Ghibel-
lines switching sides, like being expelled from

school as a way of exorcism. Poetry is exorcism,
love is a drive to the dripstone, dying in flakes.

69

If we metabolize the nightcap, all the insomnia of
green dragons and indissoluble writers, what we

end up with are a few keepsakes that mesmerize
the ignorant afternoon sunshine in blueshift mode.

70

Your blurb is capital-intensive. I want to be cooked,
decubitis with lumbar puncture, rescued in your esti-

mation, a gaggle of frontispieces, admitting my loss-
es, antithesis of Lorenzo de' Medici, nightcrawler.

About the Author

Anis Shivani is a poet, fiction writer, and literary critic living in Houston, Texas. His critically acclaimed books include *Anatolia and Other Stories*, *The Fifth Lash and Other Stories*, *Karachi Raj: A Novel*, *My Tranquil War and Other Poems*, *Whatever Speaks on Behalf of Hashish: Poems*, *Soraya: Sonnets*, *Against the Workshop: Provocations, Polemics, Controversies*, and *Literary Writing in the Twenty-First Century: Conversations*. His work appears widely in such journals as the *Yale Review*, *Georgia Review*, *Southwest Review*, *Boston Review*, *Threepenny Review*, *Michigan Quarterly Review*, *Antioch Review*, *Black Warrior Review*, *Western Humanities Review*, *Boulevard*, *Pleiades*, *AGNI*, *Fence*, *Denver Quarterly*, *The Journal*, *Gulf Coast*, *Third Coast*, *Volt*, *Subtropics*, *New Letters*, *Times Literary Supplement*, *London Magazine*, *Cambridge Quarterly*, *Meanjin*, *Fiddlehead*, *Dalhousie Review*, *Antigonish Review*, and elsewhere. He has also written for many magazines and newspapers including *Salon*, *Daily Beast*, *AlterNet*, *CommonDreams*, *Truthout*, *Huffington Post*, *Texas Observer*, *In These Times*, *Boston Globe*, *San Francisco Chronicle*, *Kansas City Star*, *Pittsburgh Post-Gazette*, *St. Petersburg Times*, *Baltimore Sun*, *Charlotte Observer*, *Austin American-Statesman*, and elsewhere. He is the winner of a Pushcart Prize, and a graduate of Harvard College.

www.ingramcontent.com/pod-product-compliance
Lightning Source LLC
Chambersburg PA
CBHW080407230426
43662CB00016B/2347